Medjugorje ... *Back in the day*

James Mulligan

Photographs by Umberto Pizzi

Published 2018

by

Soaring Eagle Press
London, EC1N 8EX

ISBN-13: 978-1717535146

ISBN-10: 1717535143

In Memoriam

BERNARD ELLIS R.I.P.

13th April 1939 – 18th June 2016

Tireless benefactor, friend and promoter of Medjugorje

THE MEDJUGORJE APPARITIONS

Since 24th June 1981 some truly astonishing happenings have been claimed to be taking place in Medjugorje, a village in a mountainous region of Bosnia-Hercegovina, just south-west of Mostar. It is claimed that the mother of Jesus, traditionally known in the Catholic Church as Our Lady, the Blessed Virgin Mary, has been appearing to six 'visionaries' and giving 'messages' to the world. Svetište Kraljice Mira, www.medjugorje.hr, the official website publishing information on Medjugorje, details the following information on the phenomenon:

On June 24, 1981, at about 6pm, six young parishioners from Medjugorje: Ivanka Ivankovic, Mirjana Dragicevic, Vicka Ivankovic, Ivan Dragicevic, Ivan Ivankovic and Milka Pavlovic, saw on the hill Crnica (on the place called Podbrdo) an apparition, a white form with a child in her arms. Surprised and scared, they did not approach. The next day at the same time, June 25, 1981, four of them, Ivanka Ivankovic, Mirjana Dragicevic, Vicka Ivankovic and Ivan Dragicevic, felt strongly drawn towards the place where, the day before, they saw the One who they had recognised as Our Lady. Marija Pavlovic and Jakov Colo joined them. The group of Medjugorje visionaries was formed. They prayed with Our Lady and talked to Her. From that day onward, they had daily apparitions, together or separately. Milka Pavlovic and Ivan Ivankovic have never seen Our Lady any more.

Mirjana Dragicevic-Soldo was born on March 18th, 1965, in Sarajevo. She had daily apparitions until December 25th, 1982. On that day, entrusting to her the tenth secret, Our Lady told her that for the rest of her life she would have one yearly apparition, on March 18th. Since August 2nd, 1987, on each second day of the month, she hears interiorly Our Lady's voice and prays with her for unbelievers. Sometimes she also sees her. Mirjana is married, she has two children, and she lives with her family in Medjugorje. The prayer intention that Our Lady confided her: for unbelievers, those who have not come to know the love of God.

Ivanka Ivankovic-Elez was born on June 21st, 1966, in Bijakovici, in the parish of Medjugorje. She was the first one who saw Our Lady. She had daily apparitions until May 7th, 1985. On that day, confiding to her the tenth secret, Our Lady told her that for the rest of her life, she would have one yearly apparition on June 25th, the anniversary of the apparitions. Ivanka is married, she has three children, and she lives with her family in Medjugorje. The prayer intention that Our Lady confided her: for families.

Jakov Colo was born on March 6th, 1971, in Sarajevo. He had daily apparitions from June 25th, 1981 to September 12th, 1998. On that day, entrusting to him the tenth secret, Our Lady told him that forthe rest of his life he would have one yearly apparition, on Christmas Day. Jakov is married, he has three children, and he lives with his family in Medjugorje. The prayer intention that Our Lady confided him: for the sick.

Ivan Dragicevic was born on May 25th, 1965 in Bijakovici, in the parish of Medjugorje. He still has daily apparitions. Our Lady entrusted nine secrets to him. Ivan is married and he has three children. With his family, he lives in the USA and in Medjugorje. The prayer intention that Our Lady confided him: for young people and for priests.

Vicka Ivankovic-Mijatovic was born on September 9th, 1964, in Bijakovici, in the parish of Medjugorje. She still has daily apparitions. Our Lady entrusted nine secrets to her. Vicka is married, has one child and lives in Krehin Gradac near Medjugorje. The prayer intention that Our Lady confided her: for the sick.

Marija Pavlovic-Lunetti was born on April 1st, 1965, in Bijakovici, in the parish of Medjugorje. She still has daily apparitions. Through her, Our Lady gives her message to the parish and the world. From March 1st, 1984, to January 8th, 1987, the message was given every Thursday, and since January 1987, on every 25th of the month. Our Lady entrusted nine secrets to her. Marija is married and she has four children. With her family, she lives in Italy and in Medjugorje. The prayer intention that Our Lady confided her: for the souls in purgatory.

A FORESHADOWING OF THE MEDJUGORJE APPARITIONS?

Years before the drama of Medjugorje began it seems intimations of the extraordinary events-to-be in Medjugorje had been around. This is particularly indicated in the construction of a huge concrete cross on the larger of the two hills overlooking the hamlets. Originally named Šipovac (Rosehip Hill), its name was changed to Križevac (Hill of the Cross) after the erection of a large reinforced-concrete crucifix there in 1933. The driving force behind the construction of the cross on Križevac was the then parish priest of Medjugorje, Fr Bernardin Smoljan, a priest of determination and tenacity, who enthused and cajoled his parishioners into the awesome task of carrying stones, steel, cement and wood up the rocky, thorn-strewn 1,500ft high hill to erect the impressive 30ft high cross on the summit to commemorate the 1900th anniversary of the death and resurrection of Jesus. Apparently the women of the village responded initially more enthusiastically than the men!

Fr Bernardin Smoljan
... he was murdered by the Communists at Mostar in 1945

The cross was completed early in 1934 and the first Mass offered on Križevac on March 15th, 1934. The following is written on the cross:

TO JESUS CHRIST, THE REDEEMER OF THE HUMAN RACE,

AS A SIGN OF OUR FAITH, LOVE AND HOPE

IN MEMORY OF THE 1900th ANNIVERSARY OF THE PASSION OF JESUS

Fr Grgo Vasilj who offered the first Mass on Križevac. He, like Fr Bernardin Smoljan, was also murdered by the Communists in Mostar in 1945

The first Mass on Križevac, celebrated on March 15th, 1934. Our Lady told the visionaries that the cross on Križevac was in God's plan for Medjugorje.

Almost every able-bodied person in the parish climbed the hill on the day of consecration and of this first Mass, which was celebrated at the foot of the cross by Fr Grgo Vasilj. Since then it has become a tradition to celebrate Holy Mass at the base of the cross on the first Sunday after September 8th, the

Sunday dedicated to celebrating the Exaltation of the Cross. One of the consequent blessings Medjugorje villagers believe bestowed was that the devastating hailstorms, which hitherto frequently destroyed the vineyard harvests, ceased completely.

Among Fr Bernardin Smoljan's other plans had been a project to build a new church, because the existing one was much damaged by subsidence, but in the dire poverty of the 1930s this was impossible and it would be the late Sixties before a new church was consecrated in Medjugorje. When in 1969 the new church was completed it was much too large for local needs and villagers began to wonder why they had built such a large church.

**The old church in Medjugorje completed in 1897 after the creation of the parish in 1892.
It became damaged beyond repair by subsidence.**

A celebration at the unfinished new church of St James in Medjugorje in 1966

St James' church in Medjugorje, consecrated on January 19th 1969,
as it was prior to the apparitions which began on 24th June 1981.

Medjugorje 1981

Tending the vineyards around the time of the beginning of the apparitions

The Medjugorje visionaries:

Left to right Mirjana Dragićević, Vicka Ivanković, Ivanka Ivanković,
Ivan Dragićević, Marija Pavlović   *Front:* Jakov Čolo

The Medjugorje visionaries photographed during an apparition in 1981

Detailed Description of Our Lady, the Queen of Peace, as she appears in Medjugorje

Over the years people questioned the visionaries of Medjugorje about Our Lady's appearance, but the most successful inquirer by far was the author, Fr. Janko Bubalo, a Franciscan of the Hercegovinian province. He had followed the events associated with the apparitions from the beginning. For a number of years he heard confessions in Medjugorje and acquired an intimate knowledge of Medjugorje spirituality. One result of his interest is his book *A Thousand Encounters with the Blessed Virgin Mary in Medjugorje* (1985). It met with worldwide success and received a reward. In this book Vicka, the visionary, in answer to Fr. Bubalo's questions, gives a detailed account of her encounters with Our Blessed Lady. It is true that Fr. Bubalo had interviews with the other visionaries, but in the end decided to publish only the conversations he had with Vicka, because it seemed to him that she answered his questions in the most comprehensive way. Besides, what the other visionaries had to say did not differ essentially from Vicka's accounts.

Time has passed and attempts at portraying Our Lady as she appears at Medjugorje have multiplied. Many of these attempts diverged from the description given by the visionaries, so in order to prevent from further confusion, Fr. Bubalo, though now advanced in years (he was born in 1913), sent a questionnaire to all the visionaries in which he asked them to supply answers to a number of questions relating to Our Lady's appearance. Five of the six visionaries responded to Fr. Bubalo appeal and signed their completed questionnaire forms at Humac in 1992. These five were Ivan Dragićević, Vicka Ivanković, Marija Pavlović, Ivanka Ivanković and Mirjana Dragićević. Because of circumstances, the sixth visionary, Jakov Čolo was unable to return his questionnaire form, but he agreed with what the other visionaries said, and had nothing to add to their accounts.

The questions and the visionaries' brief answers.

1. As the first thing, tell me: how tall is the Madonna that you regularly see?
About 165 cm - Like me. (Vicka) [5 feet 5 inches]

2. Does she look rather "slender", slim or . . .?
She looks rather slender.

3. About how many kilograms do you think she weighs?
About 60 kilograms (132 pounds).

4. About how old do you think she is?
From 18 to 20 years old.

5. When she is with the Child Jesus does she look older?
She looks as usual - she looks the same.

6. When Our Lady is with you is she always standing or . . .
Always standing.

7. On what is she standing?
On some little cloud.

8. What colour is that little cloud?
The cloud is a whitish color.

9. Have you ever seen her kneel?
Never! (Vicka, Ivan, Ivanka. . .)

10. Naturally your Madonna also has her own face. How does it look: round or rather long - oval?
It's rather long - oval - normal.

11. What colour is her face?
Normal - rather light - rosy cheeks.

12. What colour is her brow?
Normal - mainly light like her face.

13. What kind of lips does Our Lady have - rather thick or thin?
Normal - beautiful - they are more thin.

14. What colour are they?
Reddish - natural colour.

15. Does Our Lady have any dimples, as we people usually have?
Ordinarily she doesn't - perhaps a little, if she smiles. (Mirjana)

16. Is there some pleasant smile ordinarily noticeable on her countenance?
Maybe - more like some indescribable gentleness - there's a smile visible as if somehow under her skin. (Vicka)

17. What is the colour of Our Lady's eyes?
Her eyes are wonderful! Clearly blue. (all)

18. Are they rather big or . . .?
More normal - maybe a little bit bigger. (Marija)

19. How are her eyelashes?
Delicate - normal.

20. What colour are her eyelashes?
Normal - no special colour.

21. Are they thinner or . . .?
Ordinary - normal.

22. Of course, Our Lady also has a nose. What is it like: sharp or . . .?
A nice, little nose (Mirjana) - normal, harmonizing with her face. (Marija)

23. And Our Lady's eyebrows?
Her eyebrows are thin - normal - more of a black colour.

24. How is your Madonna dressed?
She is clothed in a simple woman's dress.

25. What colour is her dress?
Her dress is grey - maybe a little bluish-grey. (Mirjana)

26. Is the dress tight-fitting or does it fall freely?
It falls freely.

27. How far down does her dress reach?
All the way down to the little cloud on which she's standing - it blends into the cloud.

28. How far up around the neck?
Normally - up to the beginning of her neck.

29. Is a part of Our Lady's neck visible?
Her neck is visible, but nothing of her bosom is visible.

30. How far do her sleeves reach?
Up to her palms.

31. Is Our Lady's dress hemmed with anything?
No, not with anything.

32. Is there anything pulled in or tied around Our Lady's waist?
No, there's nothing.

33. On the body of the Madonna that you see, is her femininity noticeable?
Of course it's noticeable! But nothing specially. (Vicka)

34. Is there anything else on Our Lady besides this dress described?
She has a veil on her head.

35. What colour is that veil?
The veil is a white colour.

36. Pure white or . . .?
Pure white.

37. How much of her does the veil cover?
It covers her head, shoulders and complete body from the back and from the sides.

38. How far down does it reach?
It reaches down to the little cloud, also like her dress.

39. How far does it cover in front?
It covers from the back and from the sides.

40. Does the veil look firmer, thicker than Our Lady's dress?
No it doesn't - it's similar to the dress.

41. Is there any kind of jewellery on her?
There is no kind of jewellery.

42. Is the veil trimmed with anything at the ends?
Not with anything.

43. Does Our Lady have any kind of ornament at all?
She has no kind.

44. For example, on her head or around the head?
Yes - she has a crown of stars on her head.

45. Are there always stars around her head?
Ordinarily there are - there always are. (Vicka)

46. For example, when she appears with Jesus?
She's the same way.

47. How many stars are there?
There are twelve of them.

48. What colour are they?
Golden - gold colour.

49. Are they in any way connected with each other?
They are connected with something - so that can stay up. (Vicka)

50. Is a little bit of Our Lady's hair visible?
A little bit of her hair is visible.

51. Where do you see it?
A little above her forehead - from under the veil - from the left side.

52. What colour is it?

Its black.

53. Is either of Our Lady's ears ever visible?

No, they are never visible.

54. How is that?

Well, the veil covers her ears.

55. What is Our Lady usually looking at during the apparition?

Usually she is looking at us - sometimes at something else, at what she's showing.

56. How does Our Lady hold her hands?

Her hands are free, relaxed, extended.

57. When does she hold her hands folded?

Almost never - maybe sometimes at the "Glory be".

58. Does she ever move, gesture with her hands during the apparitions?

She does not gesture, except when she shows something.

59. Which way are her palms turned when her hands are extended?

Her palms are usually relaxed upwards - her fingers are relaxed in the same way.

60. Are her fingernails then also visible?

They are partially visible.

61. How are they - which colour are they?

Natural colour – clean-cut fingernails.

62. Have you ever seen Our Lady's legs?

No - never - her dress always covers them.

63. Finally, is Our Lady really beautiful, as you have said?

Well, really we haven't told you anything about that - her beauty cannot be described - it is not our kind of beauty - that is something ethereal - something heavenly - something that we'll only see in Paradise - and then only to a certain degree.

The first photo taken of the Medjugorje visionaries.
This photo taken on the hillside of Podbrdo (Apparition Hill), Medjugorje on 28th June 1981.

ST JAMES' CHURCH, MEDJUGORJE 1981

MEDJUGORJE 1984

Umberto Pizzi

Umberto Pizzi in Medjugorje in January 1984

Born in 1937, Umberto Pizzi became a photojournalist in 1963. He has worked in Iraq, Iran, Turkey, Syria and Jordan. He has for many years recorded the Italian social and political scene in Rome.

Fr James Mulligan is Parish Priest of St Paul's Parish in the Roman Catholic Archdiocese of Westminster in London. He is also chaplain to the Harefield Heart and Lung Hospital.

Marija Pavlović

Ivan Dragićević

Jakov Čolo

Fra Slavko Barbarić

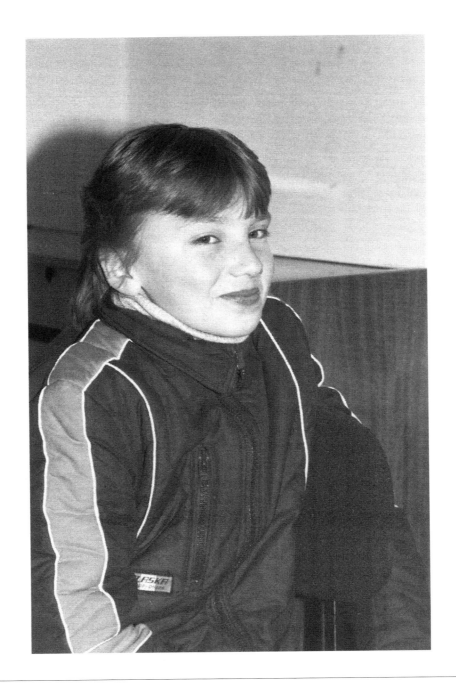

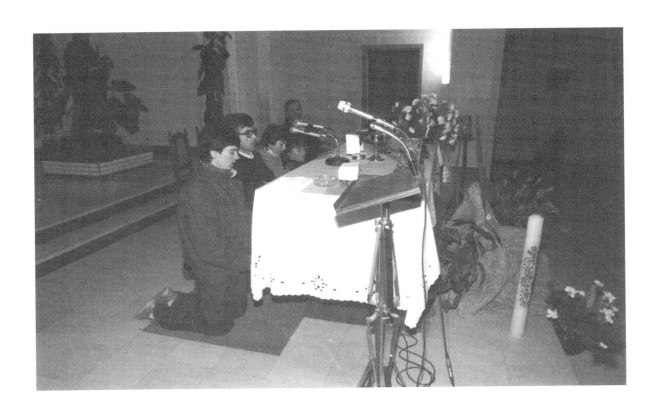

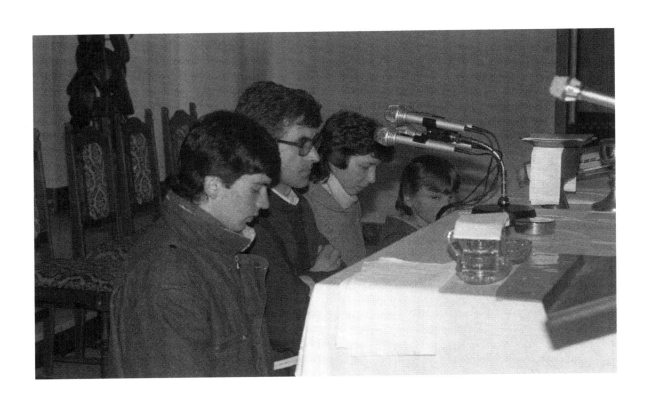

BERNARD ELLIS R.I.P.

13th April 1939 - 18th June 2016

Born into the Orthodox Jewish faith, the British businessman, Bernard Ellis, was without question one of the most active benefactors and supporters of Medjugorje anywhere in the world. He married his wife Sue in 1968 and they had five children - twelve grandchildren so far! Bernard was received into the Catholic Church in 1987.

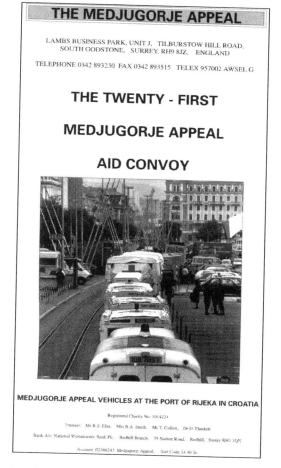

Bernard Ellis organized regular aid convoys to Croatia and Bosnia-Herzegovina during the Balkans War 1991 - 1995

Bernard and Sue Ellis in the early years of their marriage

Bernard Ellis interviewed by Fr James Mulligan 28th October 2009

On 28th October 2009, at his home in leafy Bletchingly in Surrey, England, Bernard spoke to Fr James Mulligan about his involvement with Medjugorje.

Bernard Ellis, Marija Pavlović-Lunetti and Sue Ellis in Medjugorje, September 2009

JM: Bernard you came to the Catholic faith through Medjugorje. Can you tell us how this happened?

Bernard Ellis: *As I look back it is certainly true that Medjugorje brought me into the Catholic Church, but the journey really began with my meeting my wife Sue in the 1960s. We met at the Whisky A Go-Go night club in London's Soho! Sue, daughter of the famous boxer Dave Crowley, had been a dancer (a dancer who wore clothes I hasten to add!) in the Windmill Theatre. This hardly sounds the scenario for first steps to the Catholic religion – but Sue developed into a lady of great faith, someone always searching for deeper understanding of the faith, and I was brought along on her journey.*

But as to how Medjugorje came about: in August 1983 we went on holiday to Dubrovnik – a little bit of subterfuge here by Sue who had been interested in Medjugorje, and knew that if we were in Dubrovnik a visit to Medjugorje was a possibility. Anyhow, to cut a long story short, we did arrive in Medjugorje, and Sue and I found ourselves standing with the large crowds waiting for a chance to see the visionaries as they arrived for the evening apparitions, which in those days took place in a room off from the church sanctuary. Then something quite incredible happened: from the large numbers imploring to be allowed into the small room to be present at the apparitions, Fr Tomislav Pervan came out and hustled myself and an Italian lady across the sanctuary and into this room. The room was small and very crowded. It was unbearably hot. There were people squeezed shoulder to shoulder, and there wasn't an inch to spare. Soon the six visionaries came in. They started to pray, and then they fell to their knees. I was looking at the wall to see if I could see anything unusual, but I just saw the wall and a rather badly painted statue of the Virgin Mary. As everybody knelt, so did I - there was no alternative. (This was the first occasion that I was forced to kneel. By tradition Jewish people do not kneel for fear that they would be breaking one of the Commandments by bowing down in front of a graven image, which is contrary to the Orthodox Jewish teachings that I had received when I was a young man.) We were packed so tightly together that when one knelt down we all had to kneel down. I remember thinking that it was impossible for any more people to get in the room. Standing up, it was crowded enough, but kneeling down we were taking up twice the space. So there was a knee in my calf, and there was another knee on my heel and I felt most uncomfortable. The room was silent - just the sound of the people breathing and then the silence was broken by the sound of crying - it was the Italian lady who carried a sick child. I began to notice that there was some special presence, something was happening in that room which I didn't understand. And then before I knew where I was, and what was happening, everybody was standing up and we were outside. My wife was waiting, with tears streaming down her face, saying to me, "You'll never know just what a wonderful grace this has been for all of our family." Sue was so overwhelmed and happy that I had been in the room of the apparitions.

Over the following years there were many more visits to Medjugorje. The graces continued to flow to me, and I decided God was calling me to baptism and the Catholic faith. I was received into the Catholic Church, confirmed and baptised and received my first Holy Communion on Thursday, 13th April 1987. Coincidentally, it was also the first night of the Jewish Passover. The first night of the Jewish Passover and Holy Thursday does not always fall on the same day, but on this year it did. For Jewish people the Messiah will come on the first night of the Passover; it's a tradition and they wait for the Messiah to come on that night. For me the Messiah did come on that night when I was baptized, confirmed and received my first Holy Communion. There was one extra little gift which I'm sure was a present from our Blessed Mother. This momentous day for me, the 13th April 1987, also happened to be my birthday. I'm sure it was a gift from the Blessed Mother who had been calling me. She had arranged for this day to coincide with my birthday. Born again on my birthday. What a wonderful grace for this Jewish man! During the years that followed I visited Medjugorje on many occasions, and I became very friendly with all the Franciscans: Fr Ivan Landeka, Fr Leonard Orec, Fr Tomislav Pervan, Fr Svet and Fr Slavko - who were always so welcoming to me, accepting me as a Jewish man who had become a Catholic through his Medjugorje experience. I had the privilege of getting to know Father Slavko closely. He had a great love for the Jewish people and was always interested in their history and culture.

Always hands on: Bernard replacing a wheel on a Medjugorje aid convoy truck in 1994

When the Balkan Wars broke out in 1991, I formed a charity in England which, through the generosity of the people of this country, delivered over twenty million pounds worth of aid to the whole of Croatia and Bosnia-Hercegovina. We wanted to help those people who had helped us so much by their examples of faith, hospitality and friendship. Apart from food and medical supplies we delivered one hundred and sixty vehicles which were left in the region so that the local people could assist themselves by delivering aid and medical supplies to remote areas where it was most needed, and to places which were in the midst of dreadful fighting.

JM: This charity endeavour made you a central target when a Channel 4 television documentary in Britain made very damaging allegations about how it was conducted. Could you describe how all this came about, Bernard?

Bernard Ellis: *The formation of the British charity – The Medjugorje Appeal – was never planned, it just evolved. At the beginning of the war, Father Svet was the chaplain to the Franciscan Sisters in the Mostar region. Their convent was bombed and destroyed, and about ninety nuns, some very elderly and some physically unwell, were homeless. Father Svet placed these sisters in ones and twos with the local community spread all over Mostar. Shortly after this his car was stolen, and he was unable to keep in touch with them and be the link to keeping them in touch with one another. Father Svet asked if I could help by getting him a car – which I did. This became known of in Medjugorje, and I had requests for an ambulance to help the local people, and three Landrovers for the delivery of aid and food to areas under attack. The work took off from there and eventually the charity, The Medjugorje Appeal, was formed and registered with the Charity Commissioners. I then advertised for volunteers. Men and women came forward from every walk of life. Students in their gap year to retired people, doctors, nurses, bus drivers, firemen, business people, housewives, factory workers, every walk of life and every age. The vast majority had never driven across Europe in a convoy. Initiatives to form convoys were undertaken by London Transport, Sotheby's the auction house, Cambridge University, Yorkshire Police and many other groups of people including one that formed an all-women driver convoy. The British horse racing industry sponsored a race meeting at Lingfield Park racecourse to raise money, and many famous trainers and jockeys took part in a convoy, which in their case consisted or horseboxes being loaded up with aid and returning empty. The Medjugorje Appeal purchased a surplus coach which travelled with each convoy to bring back the drivers after they had delivered their vehicles, and eventually the coach was left in Medjugorje for use by a local school. As well as The Medjugorje Appeal's initiative to supply vehicles to the region, we collected medical and food supplies in a warehouse in Godstone and two to four container loads of aid were shipped each week throughout the war period. A total of in the region of twenty million pounds worth of medical supplies, food and vehicles were delivered.*

But of course, human nature being what it is, divisions arose within The Medjugorje Appeal – wrangling, jealousies, maneuverings, backbiting. Some of the disaffected took their story to someone who sold this for money (£10,000 actually) to a television production company, Clark Television, and in 1997 a documentary on our charity was broadcast on the Channel 4 Dispatches programme. Some very damaging allegations were made (all by implication and innuendo) - among them that monies donated for the relief of war refugees at Medjugorje had been misappropriated to fund arms for the Croatian National Army. It was devastating – especially as I and Fr Slavko had thought these people were making a programme positive about our work. May God forgive those who brought about this treachery. I believe that this has played heavily on their consciences, because I feel some of them were genuinely shocked when they saw the seriousness and falsehood of the allegations. Anyhow, the allegations that emanated from the Channel 4 Dispatches programme were investigated by the Charity Commission who found that there was no evidence whatsoever that anything untoward took place, and The Medjugorje Appeal was completely exonerated. I was personally cleared and free to organise any registered charity in the future, should I wish to do so. Of course the vindication came two months after the programme was shown and, as is so often the case here, people tend to remember the original allegations, but they usually do not get to hear of the exoneration. I'm not ashamed to say that all this did cause me a lot of stress – but then perhaps insignificant suffering compared with those over the centuries who have had to lay down their very lives for the faith. Some people will continue to believe that there is no smoke without fire. But as for me, I know that many people were helped and many lives were saved, and if I ever had the opportunity to do the same thing again, I would - even if it meant a public criticism…It was five years after these allegations - during which time, all my business interests fell apart - before I could say I was back on even keel.

JM: Bernard you had a great friendship with the late Fr Slavko. How do you remember him best?

Bernard Ellis: *We spent a great deal of time together. It must have been a strange thing for many people that Father Slavko and I could have formed such a friendship because our personalities and backgrounds were so different. Father Slavko once said to me: "When I ask you to help, you always say 'yes' straight away. You never ask what I want you to do. You just say 'yes', I will help. You know instinctively that I would not ask you to do anything that you could not do. Bernard, you are a true friend." These were very treasured words for me.*

One experience that Fr Slavko recounted to me reveals so much of the priest he was. This occurred during the darkest days of the Croatian Homeland War when Serb troops were at the very threshold of Medjugorje, at the rear of Apparition Hill. His spirit was understandably downcast – although as a man of faith he never lost hope. The incident he described was, he felt, a small glimpse given to him reinforcing the conviction of our faith that hope should never fade. Fr Slavko, as many will know, was a tireless worker in the Lord's vineyard. I think he got about four hours sleep a night. And this was on a makeshift bed on a collapsible sofa in the Medjugorje presbytery living room. He was always up before day break, and out praying on Apparition Hill or Križevac. Anyhow, on this morning during the worst of the Homeland War, he went out and climbed to the top of Križevac. It was pitch dark and a storm was blowing and torrential rain bucketing down – as it can do only in Medjugorje. He reached the Cross at the summit of Križevac. It was still pitch black dark. And there, just close to where he died some years later, near the Cross was the welcoming glow of a small candle that had remained alight all night despite the gales and the torrential rain. This was deeply symbolic for him. He felt that if this little candle could keep its flame alive all night in such conditions, then he could keep the flame of hope alive in his heart, no matter how bleak things may look at any moment.

Father Slavko is undoubtedly a saint - but he was not a plaster saint. This was a real man who did not mind getting his hands dirty with a task, and who was very human. I have great memories of him here in this house in Bletchingly. This was during the Balkan Wars in 1991 – 1995 on his visits to Britain, and he would come back in the evenings and sit on the edge of the sofa watching the television news for

One of Bernard Ellis's prized possessions: an oil painting of Fr Slavko Barbarić.
It was painted in 2005 by Fr Slavko's nephew, Ivan Barbarić.

The Medjugorje visionary Marija Pavlović at Bernard Ellis' home in Bletchingly

the latest on the war situation. He would have a glass of whisky in one hand and a cigarette in the other. (Yes, he did have the occasional whisky, but only after he had finished his public commitments, and yes, he did smoke the odd cigarette, but always in private. I think even saints are allowed this!) As I said, Fr Slavko was not a remote, pious, plaster saint. Many have memories of seeing Fr Slavko regularly at daybreak on Krizevac with a plastic bag picking up litter left by pilgrims. He was truly Franciscan at heart, and was very much in the Balkan Franciscan tradition. And, believe me, this is a tough lifestyle that these Balkan Franciscans endure. I stayed once at the Franciscan monastery at Split in 1993. I experienced briefly their daily routine. In the morning all washed at a communal trough. They shaved in cold water with just a razor and carbolic soap. Not even a mirror. And no heat despite the fact that we were in the middle of a freezing cold winter. This is not a life for any namby pamby. Yes, Fr Slavko, God rest his soul, was human - but was also the most selfless person I have ever known. His death left everyone connected with Medjugorje in deep shock.

JM: Bernard, you are back in business now – and thank God for that since your business acumen has been such an asset to Medjugorje over the years. You never fear of a conflict between God and Mammon?

Bernard Ellis: *No. One of the most repeated misquotations from Scripture is that Saint Paul said: 'Money is the root of all evil.' He said no such thing. He said: 'The love of money is the root of all evil.' Very different. Money itself should not be the object nor desire of anyone's life. But if money does come along, it is how the money is used that is the important thing. Among other business interests, at the moment I am involved in selling apartments in Medjugorje. A friend of mine decided to build sixteen apartments in Medjugorje but couldn't sell them. He asked me to help. Before I got involved, I asked the parish priest his opinion on foreigners owning apartments in Medjugorje, and he told me I did not need to ask his approval but his opinion was that is was a good thing, and that Medjugorje was a place which should be available to everybody. (Not all the Franciscans subsequently agreed with this by the way.) I advertised the apartments, and very quickly all sixteen were sold. A builder friend of mine decided to build some more, and I have been involved in this venture. These apartments mean many relatives and friends of the owners can spend time in Medjugorje. People buy second homes all over the world, and can you think of a better place to own a second home than in Medjugorje? Indeed, people own properties in Lourdes, Fatima, Jerusalem and other holy places - and why not?*

JM: Could you describe your day to day work in the Medjugorje Apostolate?

There are many people in this country who assist with spreading the messages received by the visionaries and communicating information on Medjugorje. I am just one of them. My wife Sue and I circularise books about Medjugorje, and promote Medjugorje as best we can. We have here in our local parish recitation of the Rosary before Mass, and Eucharistic Adoration once a week. I also write to the press whenever the press publish something that is factually incorrect, and try to set the record straight - and very often this involves the Catholic press. The misinformation spread about Medjugorje (and often very deliberately) is something unsettling to observe. Also I speak about the apparitions in Medjugorje openly and without any embarrassment anywhere I am – airports often provide an ideal venue. Before I became a Catholic, I was embarrassed, say at an airport, about admitting to visiting Medjugorje and would say I was going to Croatia on business or something like that. Now I broadcast Medjugorje to anyone I meet - anywhere. Some people say I talk too much. Maybe, but it's a wonderful way to evangelise, and I cannot help giving my witness.

Bernard with the Medjugorje priest Fra Svetozar Kraljevic OFM

St Vincent's Centre
Carlisle Place
London SW1P 1NL

Tel: 020 7592 1850
Fax: 020 7592 1870

info@passage.org.uk
www.passage.org.uk

Registered charity number
1079764

Founding Patron
Cardinal Basil Hume

Patron
Archbishop Vincent Nichols

18th July 2016

My dear Sue,

We brought our group from The Passage to Chartwell (Lingfield SVP) last week. While there Angelina told me the sad news of Bernard's death. I am writing this note to express my deep sadness and sympathy with you on this huge loss. I am so sorry.

Bernard was such a remarkable man, so full of life and song and fun. He had a terrific capacity to set a group a-fire with life and joy. I recall those visits to Caterham and, on occasion, to the farm for an overnight. Sometimes we were gathered and somewhat at a loss until Bernard arrived. In a few minutes the group would become infected by the joy, fun and love so characteristic of Bernard.

I cannot imagine what a gap this has left in your and your childrens' lives. I shall offer the Mass that I celebrate here at The Passage with our clients (some of whom will remember Bernard) this Wednesday. May the gracious Lord of life, whose Spirit so imbued Bernard receive him into the Light of his face. And may that same Lord of life console you in your time of grief.

Sincerely,

Padraig Regan, CM.

15th August 2008

My Darling Sue,

In two days time we will celebrate forty years of marriage and a friendship which goes back to 1961 so we have know each other 47 years. I have no doubt that God brought us together as he knew we needed each other and that by his grace and with his ever loving care, many good things would happen. They did, and if you look back over the years you will see periods where we were lost to the world but these moments are outshone by great miracles of God allowing us to do many things for his glory. There are too many to mention but just a few seem to come into my mind,

Our children and grandchildren and we can be proud of them and the wonderful contributions they each make for the good of others,
The work we did together in answer to our blessed Mothers call in Medjugorje,
The Medjugorje Appeal
Our Book Ministry and the hundred of thousands of books we distributed together,
Your care for Val one of Gods little children,
Your prison visits,
The work we did with the SVP and the homeless from London,
Helping with Fr. Rookey's Healing Ministry,
Arranging together Visits of priests and visionaries to England,
The day of prayer at Aylesford,
Saying the rosary at the church,
Arranging Eucharistic Adoration at our church,
Spreading the word by handing out medals, card and books wherever you could
Being nice to the people we meet,

There are many other things but in all of them we did them together and we each contributed with love to help the other answer Gods call. We are truly blessed that we were given the chance to prove to God that we love Him and were willing to help in any way we could.

I love you my darling Sue and I always have since we first met. When I look round at other men's wives I realise that I am truly blessed that we were brought together and that I have by Gods grace the prize above "rubies"

Here is a small token of my love and grateful thanks for you having said "yes" to me all those years ago. I hope you like it and I hope it fits but it's just a token and what is far more important and what I do want you to know is that I am truly thankful to you and God for all the years of loving care and friendship, for the lovely family you gave me, for the years of shopping, cleaning, cooking, fetching and carrying, for the fun we have had together, the friendship, sharing everything, and laughing and loving

In the words of Maurice Chevalier

Ah"Yes" remember it well!

With all my Love

Your

XX

A letter sent by Bernard to Sue on their fortieth wedding anniversary

A self-portrait drawing by Bernard presented to Sue on their fortieth wedding anniversary

Printed in Great Britain
by Amazon